and Flag Officer Careers

Consequences of Increased Tenure

Harry J. Thie
Margaret C. Harrell
Clifford M. Graf II
Jerry M. Sollinger

Prepared for the
Office of the Secretary of Defense

National Defense Research Institute

RAND

The research described in this report was sponsored by the Office of the Secretary of Defense (OSD). The research was conducted in RAND's National Defense Research Institute, a federally funded research and development center supported by the OSD, the Joint Staff, the unified commands, and the defense agencies under Contract DASW01-95-C-0059.

Library of Congress Cataloging-in-Publication Data

General and flag officer careers : consequences of increased tenure / Harry J. Thie ... [et al.].
    p. cm.
    "Prepared for the Office of the Secretary of Defense by RAND's National Defense Research Institute."
    "MR-868-OSD."
    Includes bibliographical references.
    ISBN 0-8330-2526-0
    1. United States—Armed Forces—Officers. 2. United States—Armed Forces—Appointments and retirements. I. Thie, Harry. II. United States. Dept. of Defense. Office of the Secretary of Defense. III. National Defense Research Institute (U.S.)

UB413.G46 2001
355.3 ' 304 ' 0973—dc21

                                                                97-25606
                                                                    CIP

RAND is a nonprofit institution that helps improve policy and decisionmaking through research and analysis. RAND® is a registered trademark. RAND's publications do not necessarily reflect the opinions or policies of its research sponsors.

Published 2001 by RAND
1700 Main Street, P.O. Box 2138, Santa Monica, CA 90407-2138
1200 South Hayes Street, Arlington, VA 22202-5050
201 North Craig Street, Suite 102, Pittsburgh, PA 15213
RAND URL: http://www.rand.org/
To order RAND documents or to obtain additional information, contact Distribution Services: Telephone: (310) 451-7002; Fax: (310) 451-6915; Email: order@rand.org

RAND's National Defense Research Institute (NDRI) was asked to address the issues on general and flag officer career patterns raised as an item of special interest in Title V (Military Personnel Policy) in the Conference Report accompanying the National Defense Authorization Act for Fiscal Year 1997. This document provides specific data requested by Congress and assesses certain consequences of requiring general and flag officers to retire upon completion of 35 years of service.

The report examines the consequences on promotion, assignments, and tour lengths of allowing general and flag officers to serve beyond 35 years. The assessment is based on models developed at RAND for analyzing officer careers at a broad, conceptual level. This is not a comprehensive study of general and flag officer management but is limited to issues related to questions raised by Congress.

This study was sponsored by the Under Secretary of Defense for Personnel and Readiness, and it was carried out in the Forces and Resources Policy Center of RAND's National Defense Research Institute, a federally funded research and development center sponsored by the Office of the Secretary of Defense, the Joint Staff, and the defense agencies. The work was completed and provided to the sponsor in 1997.

CONTENTS

FIGURES

TABLES

BACKGROUND

Congress has long taken a keen interest in the management of officer careers. It played a major role in the Defense Officer Personnel Management Act of 1980, the legislation that currently governs officer personnel management in all services. Recently, it has turned its attention to the tenure of the most senior military personnel, the general and flag officers. Although current law permits exceptions, it requires most flag-rank officers to retire once they have 35 years of active commissioned service. Congress is concerned that the current system does not adequately prepare officers for the most senior assignments. As a result of these concerns, Congress asked the Secretary of Defense to review the career patterns of flag-rank officers. It requested specific data about average time-in-grade both when selected and when promoted as well as the length of tours. It also asked the Secretary to assess the appropriateness of mandatory retirement at 35 years.

PURPOSE AND APPROACH

The Office of the Secretary of Defense (OSD) asked RAND's National Defense Research Institute (NDRI) to report on these topics. Because we perceived greater interest in the effect of longer careers for general and flag officers, we placed our emphasis upon assessing the value of extending the tenure of general and flag officers beyond 35 years of service, specifically focusing on promotions, number of assignments, and career length. Drawing on the military services and the Defense Manpower Data Center (DMDC), we gathered information about time-in-grade and tour lengths, which appears in Table S.1. To assess the appropriateness of mandatory retirement at 35 years of service, we analyzed the value and effect of adding an additional 5 years of service to the tenure of general and flag officers. This assessment proved more complex, and we analyzed it from two aspects, which we label systemic and career path. We explored the effects of different career patterns—specifically focusing on promotions, number of assignments, and career length—from each aspect by adding 5 additional years of service to the careers of flag-rank officers in various ways. The systemic consequences are quantitative and result from applying an additional 5 years of service in different ways to a population of flag-rank officers that remains constant in number and distribution. We analyzed the effect of six options. In some cases, we added the 5 years to a single rank, i.e., O-10. In others, we spread the additional time across all ranks. The results show the average system responses to additional time with respect to time-in-grade and promotion rate. Career-path responses attempt to take into account individual careers. That is, given additional time-in-grade(s), how would assignments change? This part of the analysis demonstrates that those who rise to the top have different assignment patterns than others who do not rise. We used a conceptual flow model to assess the changes in assignments in light of the overall time permitted. Those who reach O-10 generally serve in what we call "trunk" assignments, i.e., those that lead to the highest positions. They also move through the system faster than other officers. We also analyzed what would happen if the time in these trunk positions were to be extended.

Table S.1

General and Flag Officer Time-in-Grade and Tour Lengths
(Years)

	Time-in-Grade When Selected	Time-in-Grade When Promoted	Tour Length, Joint	Tour Length, Nonjoint
O-7	4.6	5.8	1.9	1.8
O-8	1.8	2.9	2.2	2.1
O-9	(a)	2.2	2.3	2.2
O-10	(a)	2.8	2.6	2.2

[a]Only O-7 and O-8 are selected by formal promotion boards.

RESULTS

The time-in-grade for selection and promotion and the average tour lengths appear in Table S.1. The data show that the average general or flag officer spends over 4 years in grade O-6 before being selected for promotion to O-7 and spends a year on the promotion list. Those promoted to O-8 have just under 2 years in grade and spend slightly over 1 year on the promotion list. Some slight differences occur in the length of joint and nonjoint tours, but typically a tour for a flag-rank officer lasts about 2 years.

Congress has asked whether it is appropriate to require flag-rank officers to retire after 35 years of commissioned service. Provisions already exist to continue individual general and flag officers beyond 35 years of service, and the military departments routinely but sparingly exercise the exceptions. The fact that they exist and are used answers the narrow question. Officers can and do serve beyond 35 years. The larger question is whether making this the rule rather than the exception is a better course of action. Removing the limit would not necessarily lengthen time between promotions or assignments. The services could use the same career patterns they do now.

We believe the answer depends on three perspectives: that of the individual, that of the organizations in which general and flag officers serve, and that of the military service whose broad interests the general and flag officers serve over time. We assess those perspectives given a likely implementation of additional time—greater length in existing assignments (depth) rather than the introduction of more assignments (breadth) in the career path.

For the first perspective, we have no evidence of how individual general and flag officers would behave if allowed to serve longer overall and in each assignment. Officers may continue to behave as they do now: They would seek advancement to positions of responsibility, would serve as long as they were contributing, and would retire when not competitive or after 5 years of service in grade as they do now. From their perspective, they would serve in the same positions in which they do now but for somewhat longer periods. Fewer officers on average would be promoted to higher grades, and there would be greater time periods between promotions. Certain officers would be assigned to positions with greater likelihood of continued advancement, as they are now, and these officers would advance relatively more quickly than the service average.

In terms of the second perspective, the organizations (i.e., specific commands) in which general and flag officers serve would probably benefit because their leaders would serve for somewhat longer periods. Again, the same officers as now would be assigned to the same organizational positions as now, but there would be less turnover within the organization. The organizations would not be aware that promotions had slowed; they would be aware that lengths of service had increased for those general and flag officers assigned to them. Organizations would be better off to the extent that less movement than now would probably improve organizational performance. Greater length in assignments, up to a point, is generally accepted as preferable for individual and organizational effectiveness.

Third, from the perspective of the military service, the pool of officers competing for the positions of highest responsibility (moving from grade to grade) would be smaller but more experienced. It is not clear whether a service ultimately prizes depth or breadth of experience. Under our implementation assumption, the same breadth of experience would occur but with deeper experience in each assignment, which is a benefit. Overall, fewer officers would have had the opportunity to gain these experiences, which is a disadvantage. The trade-off for the service would be a smaller but more experienced pool of competitors for advancement.

Ultimately then, the answer to the question posed about the appropriateness of mandatory retirement of certain officers after 35 years of commissioned service rests in objectives. For example, if the desired outcome is greater stability overall and in particular organizations, then lifting the 35-year limit and allowing officers more routinely to serve longer in all assignments would accomplish that. If the objective is rapid movement along a career path to more important positions, then the current system accomplishes that. If the objective is to reap the benefit from having developed officers by allowing them to serve longer, then removing the 35-year limit seems best. These objectives, and others that might be put forward, sometimes conflict with each other, and decisionmakers need to decide which are the most important.

We are grateful to our sponsoring office for assistance provided as we conducted this research. In particular, Colonel Allan Brendsel, Ms. Debra McCorkle, and Major Dale Bourque shared insights about general and flag officer management with us and facilitated data collection. Each of the military services has an office that handles general and flag officer matters, and we appreciate the diligence with which they provided data and answered questions. The Defense Manpower Data Center (DMDC) was typically responsive and resourceful in providing data to meet our needs. We owe a debt of gratitude to our reviewers, Martin Binkin (formerly of The Brookings Institution) and Al Robbert of RAND, for their detailed and insightful comments. The analysis and report additionally benefited from suggestions by RAND colleagues Susan Hosek, Jim Winnefeld, and Rudy Ehrenberg. Suzanne Welt assisted us with administrative aspects of report publication.

Chapter One

INTRODUCTION

BACKGROUND

Policymakers have recently focused on the tenure of the military's most senior officers, those of general and flag rank. Legislation governing the retirement of these officers appears in Title 10 U.S. Code.[1] It stipulates that officers who have reached the two-star grade must retire either 5 years after being appointed or at 35 years of service, whichever is later.[2] If an officer has not reached the two-star level, he or she must retire 5 years after initial selection to flag rank or at 30 years, whichever is later. Some exceptions to the 35-year retirement are permitted. Officers who have achieved one- or two-star rank may be extended on active duty up to 5 years by the service secretary. Those who have reached three-star rank may also be extended for 5 years, but presidential approval is required. In neither case can officers remain on active duty beyond their 62nd birthday without presidential authority. Table 1.1 summarizes this information.

Congress exhibited keen interest in general and flag officer career patterns in the Senate authorization bill for fiscal year (FY) 97. In that legislation, Congress expressed its concern that the current process for selecting, assigning, and developing general and flag officers does not effectively prepare them for handling increasing levels of responsibility and for performing with maximum efficiency at

---

[1]Relevant language appears in Appendix A.

[2]Note that O-9s and O-10s serve in the "regular grade" of O-8 and are therefore also covered by this legislation.

Table 1.1

Age, Time-in-Grade (TIG), and Time-in-Service
(TIS) Restrictions

Grade	Max TIG	Max TIS	Max Age
O-7	5[a]	30[a]	62
O-8	5[a]	35[a]	62
O-9	5[b]	35[b]	62[c]
O-10	5[b]	35[b]	62[c]

[a]May be extended for up to 5 years by service secretary.

[b]May be extended for up to 5 years by the President.

[c]Certain assignments carry with them an automatic extension to age 64. Other officers can be extended to age 64 by the President.

each level of assignment. Specific areas of interest identified by Congress included:

- the length of time officers spend on promotion lists to grades O-7 and O-8 before they are promoted;

- the rate at which general and flag officers rotate through important positions;

- the effect of this rate both on the effectiveness of individual officers and the overall value these officers add to each position; and

- the consequences of requiring general and flag officers to retire upon completion of 35 years of service.

As a result of these concerns, Congress requested a report from the Secretary of Defense that reviewed the career patterns of general and flag officers. It asked for specific data and for an assessment of the appropriateness of retiring after 35 years of service. It asked for three specific data sets showing:

- average time-in-grade at the time of selection for promotion to each general and flag officer grade;

- average time-in-grade at the time of promotion to each general and flag officer grade; and

- average tour lengths for general and flag officers who changed positions or assignments during fiscal years 1991 through 1995.

Generally, these data were to be reported by fiscal year and by service. Where appropriate, joint duty assignments were to be addressed.

Congress also asked for an assessment of:

*   the continued appropriateness of mandatory retirement of officers after 35 years.

PURPOSE AND APPROACH

The Office of the Secretary of Defense (OSD) asked RAND's National Defense Research Institute (NDRI) to prepare the report and in particular to assess the continued appropriateness of mandatory retirement of officers after 35 years. Because we perceived greater interest in the effect of longer careers for general and flag officers, we placed our emphasis upon assessing the value of extending the tenure of general and flag officers beyond 35 years of service, specifically focusing on promotions, number of assignments, and career length. This assessment proved more complex, and we analyzed it from two aspects, which we label systemic and career path. We decided that the appropriateness of retirement after 35 years could best be evaluated if policymakers knew whether certain benefits or disadvantages would result if additional service were permitted, e.g., up to the age limit of 62 years.[3]

We determined that two principal types of consequences would occur if careers were extended beyond 35 years. The first type is quantitative, and we label it systemic. That is, in a closed personnel system with fixed overall numbers and fixed distributions at each grade, the underlying mathematics of career flow allow quantitative assessments of the number of promotions (promotion tempo), time-in-grade, and promotion expectations as anticipated length of service in grade(s) is varied in different ways. These consequences are important in that they describe average grade-related career system outcomes from allowing additional service.

---

[3]As a reference point, the Age Discrimination in Employment Act that governs age-based practices in the private sector in the United States allows for the mandatory retirement of senior executives at age 65 providing they have served at least 2 years in the senior position and they have a retirement income of at least $44,000.

A second—and more interesting—qualitative consequence deals with individual officers who move through the system in unique ways. What would officers do if they served for longer periods in particular grades? We call these career-path consequences, and they affect the number, type, and length of assignments. The general and flag officers of most interest are those who serve in important positions, i.e., those who eventually advance to the grade of O-10. The second set of consequences thus deals with an assessment of how particular career patterns, in terms of assignments, might change as time served is varied in different ways.

Additional consequences, such as the cost implications and the effect on military organizations as a result of any change in tenure restrictions, were also considered. The report does not address these consequences in detail because they are expected to be minimal, if for no other reason than that they would affect a small population. We include a brief summary here. First, it is important to remember that the same number of general and flag officer positions will still exist and thus the same number of general and flag officers will still serve. Therefore, the same number of salaries (pay and allowances) for each grade will still be paid. The pay tables for military officers extend only to 26 years of service, so there would not be a pay differential for general and flag officers who remained in service for longer than 35 years. The cost implications are likely to be marginal savings. Because fewer officers will be promoted to general and flag officer ranks if officers serve longer, more officers will retire from lower grades, so the savings would result from retirement pay at lower grades. Also, any savings (or costs) from moving individuals would result from changes in assignment patterns, not just changes in career length. For example, if longer tenure in a career enables individuals to serve in assignments for longer periods of time, there would be some potential cost savings due to a reduced number of people moving each year. If, however, the additional career time is used to add additional assignments, but the average time in assignments does not change, then there would be no cost consequences from moving. In a given year, the same number of moves would occur.

Any effect on military organizations in which general and flag officers serve will result more from the assignment policy of the services than from the tenure policy for general and flag officers. Should the tenure for these officers be extended, but assignment policy continue to rotate these officers at the same rate as now, then the change in tenure restrictions will not have any effect upon organizations (i.e., specific commands) from deeper experience. Such officers would have greater breadth of experience, however, which could increase effectiveness. Should a relaxation of tenure restriction permit longer assignments, then the organizations would enjoy greater stability in their leadership. We capture this analysis in our assessment of career-path consequences and assignment policies.

We must be clear that we are not predicting how officers' behaviors would change in response to changes in the management system. We don't know. However, what we can do is to assume and specify that certain behaviors could result from changes in the system (for example, earlier retirement for certain officers as others serve longer). Also, as discussed later, we are not assessing the effects that changing general and flag officer tenure might have on management of more junior officers.

Our approach to accomplishing this study involved a number of steps. First, we reviewed the applicable legislation and discussed it with OSD and the military services. Second, we drew on two data sources to gather statistical information about general officers. The military services provided the specific data requested by Congress, but these were point data only and did not enable us to analyze promotion distributions. So we asked the Defense Manpower Data Center (DMDC) to provide promotion histories for all officers promoted to the grades O-7 to O-10 during the period of FY 91 to FY 96.[4] These data allowed us to build distributions of promotion expecta tions around the point data provided by the services in response to the specific congressional request. These distributions gave insights into general officer promotion practices.

Third, we asked the military services to provide biographical information for all officers who had served at the grade of O-10 between FY 91 and FY 96. We used this information to assess the rate at which

---

[4]DMDC provided data by extracting records with pay grades greater than O-6 from the Verification Unified Current and Loss files through September 1996. A longitudinal file, the Work Experience File, was then used to identify changes in pay grade and to calculate the months in grade between promotions.

general and flag officers rotate through grades and through important positions, which were the ones of interest to Congress. We took important positions to be those from which officers advanced to the highest grade. We reduced the biographical data to a "trunk-and-branch" model that showed the pattern and lengths of service in positions for these officers. Using these data and the model, we varied the expected time-in-grade to determine the systemic and career-path consequences of general and flag officers serving beyond 35 years.

DOPMA AND ITS EFFECT ON OFFICER MANAGEMENT

The Defense Officer Personnel Management Act of 1980 (DOPMA) is key to understanding not only the management of general and flag officers but of the entire officer corps. The Title 10 provisions summarized above simply codify the provisions of DOPMA. Some general and service-specific aspects of DOPMA are important to understanding this study.

General Aspects of DOPMA

Three general points about DOPMA and the intent underpinning it are important here. First, general and flag officers normally cannot be considered in isolation; they are part of a larger officer corps. Indeed, in passing DOPMA, Congress concluded that general and flag officer management should be integrated with O-4 to O-6 management in a consistent manner across services.[5] So changes in field-grade officer management would normally prompt changes to the management of flag-rank officers and vice-versa. However, for this report, we assume that the management of officers in the grades of O-1 to O-6 continues as is. We assess changes only in total allowed service for the grades of O-7 to O-10. We recognize that ultimately

---

[5]"[M]any of the provisions that apply to the promotion and retirement of field grade officers have been extended to apply to general and flag officers. . . . Certain features of the general and flag officer management system will, in the committee's view, benefit from changes that conform its operation to that of the field grade management system where possible and from changes that apply the principle of consistency among the services where differences currently exist." House Report No. 96-1462, November 17, 1980.

any such changes must be integrated with the larger system of officer management. Moreover, tenure changes for general and flag officers could affect selection rates and numbers from the grade of O-6, which could have impacts on management of all officers.

Second, DOPMA passed only after several years of intense debate among the House, Senate, and the Department of Defense (DoD). The debate addressed many aspects of officer management, but of interest to this report is the reason advanced for the flag-rank officer management provisions. They were intended to increase the amount of experience ("generally provide for longer service") in officers serving as general and flag officers.[6]

Congressional interest in careers for military officers has continued. In the FY 93 Authorization Act, Congress requested a review of officer management practices and suggested that longer careers should be the rule rather than the exception. NDRI provided the review for the grades of O-1 to O-6 and sent the results to Congress in September 1994.[7] More recently, NDRI was asked to recommend a set of best officer management practices for the future given a set of desired outcomes. A recent RAND report[8] contains these recommended practices, which include a career system that fosters high turnover early in careers but longer careers overall. Such a system would be consistent with longer allowed service for general officers. It would also allow for either broader or deeper development of officers prior to selection to the grade of O-7.

A third issue is that DOPMA was designed to meet the challenges of the Cold War environment and was based in the personnel management practices of the 1970s. Its objectives and means fit less well with the current and likely future environment in which missions, strategies, organization, and technology are rapidly changing. It has

---

[6]For example, in a 1979 hearing, Senator Nunn challenged a defense witness: "The average general officer now has served only 3.7 years as a general officer—down by 25 percent from the average of 4.9 years in 1968. . . . Are you satisfied with this experience level?" Hearing before the Subcommittee on Manpower and Personnel of the Committee on Armed Services, United States Senate, July 17, 1979.

[7]Harry J. Thie, Roger A. Brown, et al., *Future Career Management Systems for U.S. Military Officers,* Santa Monica, CA: RAND, MR-470-OSD, 1994.

[8]Harry J. Thie, Margaret C. Harrell, et al., *A Future Officer Career Management System: An Objectives-based Design*, Santa Monica, CA: RAND, MR-788-OSD, 1997.

also been assessed as a better static description of the desired officer structure than as a dynamic management tool.[9] For example, while DOPMA requires general and flag ranks to retire at 35 years unless the President or Secretary of Defense grants a waiver, "these ceilings were set before joint duty requirements grabbed three to five years of an officer's career."[10] The point is that subsequent events and changes in the environment may preclude the intent of the original legislation from being accomplished.

Service-Specific Differences

Within the framework of uniform practices established by DOPMA, each service has leeway in developing—that is, educating and providing experience to—its officer corps. As a result, different career and promotion patterns can emerge that affect general officer management. For example, Navy officers in all competitive categories selected to the grade of O-7 have about 6.8 years service in grade O-6, while the average for the other services is about 5.4 years; total time-in-service at promotion is 26.9 years for the Navy and 25.4 years for the other services. Given the later promotion to O-7, Naval officers who compete with officers of other services for assignments to positions of responsibility have more service at grades before flag rank but less experience, on average, in the grades of O-7 and O-8. As a result, too few officers make flag rank soon enough either to fulfill their potential or to meet the Navy's need for senior joint and staff assignments.[11] Senior officers play catch-up to gain sufficient flag experience and still have time to serve as vice chairman or chairman of the Joint Chiefs or as a unified commander-in-chief.[12] They typically catch up by spending little or no time as O-8s. This appears to be dysfunctional because, presumably, the experience gained as O-7s and O-8s prepares one for O-9 and O-10 assignments

---

[9]Bernard Rostker, Harry J. Thie, et al., *The Defense Officer Personnel Management Act of 1980: A Retrospective Assessment*, Santa Monica, CA: RAND, R-4246-FMP, 1993.

[10]Tom Philpott, "The Navy's Pressure Cooker," U.S. Naval Institute Proceedings, May 1996, p. 50. Philpott provides a cogent review of the problems in managing current Naval officer careers and suggestions for changing such career practices.

[11]Philpott, p. 51.

[12]VADM Bowman, former Chief of Naval Personnel, as quoted in Philpott, p. 52.

better than the experience gained as captains or commanders.[13] This concern has been long-standing. Earlier RAND research identified two problems with the officer management system: It limits the amount of experience an officer can acquire as a midlevel manager (i.e., O-6 and O-7) before selection for more senior responsibilities, and it limits the time that the service can use an officer in both the middle and senior executive ranks before reaching mandatory retirement.[14]

Such service differences mean that our analysis of changes in total allowed service for general and flag officers starts at different points for each service, and one could reach different conclusions about the consequences of such additional service. We will account for these differences to some extent in our assessment.

HOW THIS REPORT IS ORGANIZED

Chapter Two contains a summary of the data provided by the services in response to the congressional direction. Chapter Two also includes additional analysis derived from the data provided by the DMDC. Chapter Three constructs a model of flag-rank mobility through important positions and assesses the consequences of changing allowed time-in-service. Chapter Four provides our conclusions. Several appendices contain additional data of interest.

---

[13]See Donald J. Cymrot, Carol S. Moore, John T. Ostlund, *The Length of Flag Careers*, Alexandria, VA: Center for Naval Analyses, CAB 95-67, September, 1995.

[14]Previous unpublished RAND research.

Chapter Two

REQUESTED DATA

CONGRESSIONAL-REQUESTED DATA

Data from each of the services appears in Appendix B. Congress requested information by service, by fiscal year (1991 through 1995), by grade, and by competitive category. Each service has different competitive categories: the Marine Corps has 1[1] and the Navy has flag officers serving in 15 different competitive categories.[2] The largest number of general and flag officers in each service is in the "line" competitive category.[3] The Army, Air Force, and Navy have separate competitive categories for health care professionals,[4] lawyers, and chaplains. The Navy's Restricted Line (RL) is a broad category made up of specific competitive categories[5] that, in the other services, are included under the line competitive category. Additionally, the

---

[1]Navy Staff Corps officers, primarily health care professionals and chaplains, are provided to the Marine Corps by the Navy. Marine Corps lawyers are included under the one broad competitive category that is used.

[2]See Table B.7.

[3]The Army calls this the Army Competitive Category. The Air Force calls it line, the Marine Corps calls it unrestricted, and the Navy calls it Unrestricted Line.

[4]The Army and the Navy have separate categories for medical doctors, dentists, nurses, and a "medical service corps" (pharmacists, hospital administrators, etc.). The Air Force has consolidated all of its health care professionals into one competitive category at the general officer level.

[5]Intelligence, cryptography, public affairs, oceanography, engineering (e.g., naval architect), and "aerospace" engineering are the Navy Restricted Line (RL) competitive categories.

Navy's Staff Corps includes two competitive categories[6] whose officers would be included under the line competitive category of the
other services. In the time-in-grade tables below, which summarize
data provided by the services and contained in Appendix B, only line
general and flag officers were used; Navy data were adjusted to include competitive categories that the Army and Air Force include
within their line category.

Time-in-Grade at the Time of Selection

Only O-7 and O-8 general and flag officers are "selected" by a for-
mally convened board; O-9s and O-10s are nominated for confirma-
tion. Also, not all O-8s were selected by a board; some staff corps
O-8s (e.g., Air Force JAG O-8 in FY 93) were appointed. Table 2.1
reflects the average time spent in the previous grade on the date the
applicable service secretary forwarded the report of the selection
board for approval/confirmation.

Table 2.1 shows wide variation between services before selection to
O-7. The Air Force and Navy tend to provide longer experience at the
O-6 level before selection to O-7 than do the Army and Marine Corps.
There is greater consistency in the time before selection to
O-8. The relatively short time between promotion to O-7 and selec-
tion to O-8 provides an early indicator to O-7s about their potential
for continued service. The average O-7 is selected for promotion to

Table 2.1

**Average Time-in-Grade at the Time of Selection (Years),
Line Generals and Flag Officers**

	Army	Air Force	Navy	Marine Corps	Average
To O-7	3.2	5.0	5.1	3.4	4.1
To O-8	1.7	2.0	1.7	1.6	1.8

NOTE: Data derived from FY91 through FY95, as requested by Congress. The
average is a weighted average reflecting the numbers of generals and flag officers
who were selected by each of the services.

---

[6]Supply Corps and Civil Engineering Corps.

O-8 in less than 2 years; an O-7 who has not been selected for promotion by then has a clear signal of diminished chances for future promotion and longer service.

Time-in-Grade at the Time of Promotion

Table 2.2 reflects the time spent in the previous grade from date of promotion at the previous grade to date of promotion at the indicated grade.

In Table 2.2, the variation between services is again apparent at the O-7 grade. The similarity between Army and Marine Corps, and Air Force and Navy, continues from selection through promotion.

The difference in time-in-grade between selection and promotion is nominally consistent for O-7 and O-8 within services.[7] It appears that general and flag selectees in all services spend approximately 1 year between selection and promotion. On average, this difference represents time spent on a promotion list.[8]

Table 2.2

**Average Time-in-Grade at the Time of Promotion (Years),
Line Generals and Flag Officers**

	Army	Air Force	Navy	Marine Corps	Average
To O-7	4.5	5.9	6.6	4.4	5.5
To O-8	3.2	3.0	2.8	2.6	2.9
To O-9	2.3	2.9	1.3	2.0	2.2
To O-10	2.4	3.3	3.0	1.8	2.8

NOTE: The average is weighted by numbers of generals and flag officers promoted.

---

[7]For example, the lag in the Marine Corps is 1.0 years for both the O-7 and the O-8 time-in-grade averages.

[8]Time spent on a promotion list would be more accurately tracked by individual than by fiscal year. In the case of this data, the officers selected and the officers promoted (which generated the data displayed in Tables 2.1 and 2.2) are not necessarily the same individuals. Moreover, we use time of promotion to a grade as the starting point for experience in that grade. If an officer is assigned to a senior position at time of selection (part of the process of "frocking"), utilization in the new grade would be greater and utilization in the previous grade would be less.

Average Tour Lengths for General or Flag Officers Who Changed Positions or Assignments

The previous two tables focus on data for those who were promoted. The data for average tour lengths, shown in Table 2.3, are derived from all who were transferred in a specific fiscal year. The tour length averages thus include tour lengths from those who were promoted to the next grade, those who remained in grade, and those who left the service.

The data indicate that, with some minimum variation, most general and flag officers spend about 2 years in assignments. The Marine Corps O-9s in joint tours had the shortest assignments, and the Marine Corps O-10s in nonjoint assignments had the longest assignments. However, these averages can be misleading in several ways. The distribution of tour lengths is not known; that is, the average could reflect tours of nominally the same duration or could reflect tours of widely varying duration. Second, the sample is constrained to 5 fiscal years; longer tours averaging close to 5 years are less likely to be captured than are tours of a shorter duration. Third, the data reflect career and assignment policies and patterns during the draw-

Table 2.3

Average Tour Lengths for General or Flag Officers Who
Changed Positions or Assignments (Years)

	Army	Air Force	Navy	Marine Corps	Average
O-7					
Joint	1.6	2.2	2.0	1.8	1.9
Nonjoint	1.6	2.0	1.9	1.7	1.8
O-8					
Joint	2.0	2.6	2.0	2.0	2.2
Nonjoint	2.0	2.2	2.2	1.8	2.1
O-9					
Joint	2.1	2.9	2.2	1.1	2.3
Nonjoint	2.4	2.3	2.2	1.7	2.2
O-10					
Joint	2.9	2.4	2.5	0.0	2.6
Nonjoint	2.1	2.0	2.2	3.1	2.2

NOTE: Average is weighted by numbers of generals and flag officers assigned/transferred.

down transition period. Moreover, O-10 averages should be viewed with caution, as there are relatively few data points.

PROMOTION DISTRIBUTIONS

As mentioned previously, our promotion data came from two sources. The services provided average time-in-grade to promotion. The DMDC provided dates of promotion and service for individual records of general and flag officers. In this section we use the promotion data of individual officers to provide additional information regarding the differences between the promotion distributions and patterns of each of the four services.

The following figures display the same data in several ways.[9] The first four figures show years in previous grade at time of promotion to the grade shown for each service. The next four figures compare years of service at the time of promotion to grades O-7 through O-10 for each service. The third set of four figures shows by military service the year in service when promotions occur to each grade. The last set of four figures shows by service the amount of promotion activity at each year of service.

Distribution of Promotions by Time-in-Grade

Figure 2.1 shows that Army and Marine Corps officers, on average, tend to spend less time at the grade of O-6 before promotion to O-7 than do officers in the Navy and Air Force. Officers in the latter two services have about 1.5 to 2 years greater experience as captains and colonels, respectively. In all services, there are about 8 years of variation between those promoted with the least time-in-grade and those promoted with the most time-in-grade. Nonline competitive categories such as medical, dental, chaplain, and judge advocate general account for many of the longer times in grade O-6 at promotion to O-7.

---

[9]This data is for promotions made in all competitive categories for fiscal years 91 to 96 and is from files maintained by the DMDC. For all services, there are 786 promotions to O-7; 519 to O-8; 230 to O-9; and 58 to O-10. By service, there are a total of 561 for the Army; 406 for the Navy; 488 for the Air Force; and 138 for the Marine Corps.

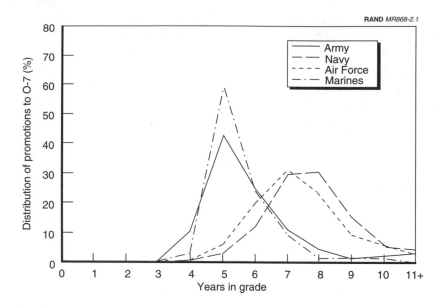

Figure 2.1—Distribution of Promotions to O-7 by Years in Grade O-6

As shown in Figure 2.2, there is far less variation in years in grade O-7 at promotion to O-8. Each service promotes to O-8, on average, after about 4 years' time in grade O-7, with most promotions occurring between 3 and 5 years in grade. While Figure 2.6 will demonstrate that some officers have fewer years of career experience than others at promotion to O-8, officers in all services tend to have about the same amount of grade experience at O-7 when they are promoted to O-8.

Figure 2.3 shows greater variance in years in grade O-8 at promotion to O-9, with the Navy promoting with the fewest years.[10] At grade O-9, individual officers are being nominated and selected for promotion to particular positions, and this process is more conducive to a broader distribution of time-in-grade. Air Force officers on average have the most experience in O-8 positions when they are promoted

---

[10]As noted elsewhere, some Navy admirals are promoted to grade O-9 with little or no time spent at grade O-8.

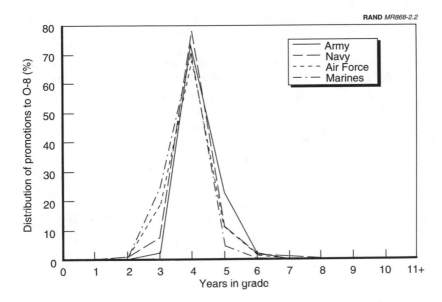

Figure 2.2—Distribution of Promotions to O-8 by Years in Grade O-7

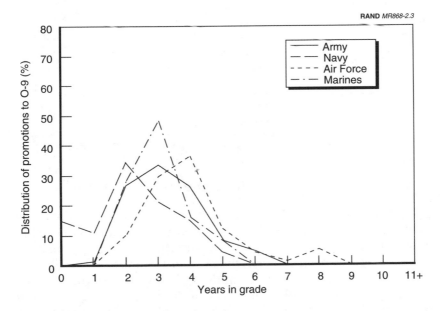

Figure 2.3—Distribution of Promotions to O-9 by Years in Grade O-8

to O-9, and Navy officers on average have the least experience in O-8 positions.

There is also variance in years in grade to O-10, as Figure 2.4 indicates. Navy and Air Force officers have the most experience in the previous grade when they are promoted to O-10. The small number of promotions in the Marine Corps contributes to the simple pattern of its promotions, but it is notable that its promotions to O-10 are completed after 3 years in grade.

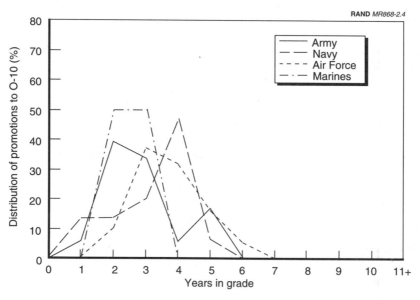

Figure 2.4—Distribution of Promotions to O-10 by Years in Grade O-9

Distribution of Promotions by Grade and Year of Service

The previous four figures looked at time-in-grade at promotion. The next four figures show time-in-service at promotion. Officers will have different years of service at promotion depending on how rapidly they advanced earlier in their careers. Some officers will have spent more cumulative time in grades O-1 through O-6 than others. These variations could result from individual differences, from higher promotion opportunities in certain services during the early career years, or from other factors.

Figure 2.5 shows that the Air Force tends to make promotions earlier in careers to the grade of O-7, while the Navy does so later in careers. Air Force O-7 promotions peak at the 25th year of service; those in the Navy do not peak until the 27th year. The Marine Corps tends to have less variation in career service at time of promotion. This pattern reflects the higher line content in the Marine Corps.

Figure 2.6 shows that most Air Force promotions to O-8 occur at 27 and 28 years of service. The Army data reveal later promotions in general than do the Air Force data, with most promotions occurring between 28 and 30 years of service. The majority of Marine Corps promotions occur within 2 years, at 28 and 29 years of service. The Navy promotes very few officers to O-8 before 29 years of service. Most Navy promotions occur with 30 and 31 years of service.

Figure 2.7 depicts the promotion distributions to grade O-9 for each of the services. The Navy and the Air Force begin promotion to O-9 earliest in careers; both promote a significant percentage of O-9s by year 28. The Army spreads most of the O-9 promotions across years

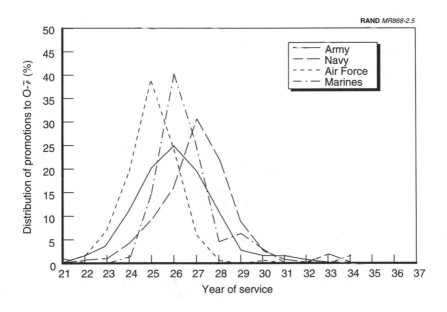

Figure 2.5—Distribution of Promotions to Grade O-7

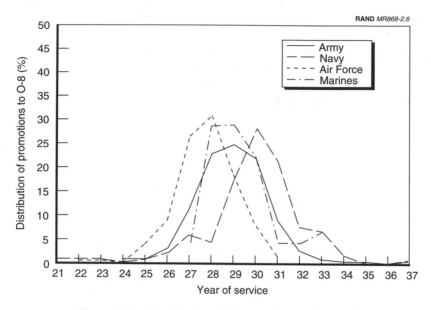

Figure 2.6—Distribution of Promotions to Grade O-8

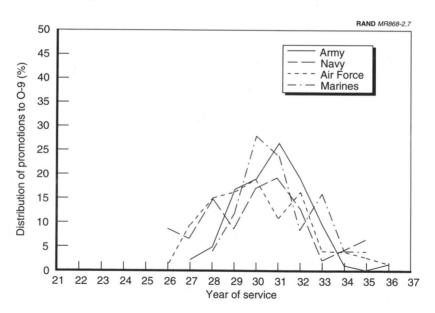

Figure 2.7—Distribution of Promotions to Grade O-9

29 to 33. While the Marine Corps starts promoting later in a career than do the other services, most of their O-9 promotions occur by year 31.

Figure 2.8 indicates that the Navy begins promotion to O-10 at year 27, earlier in a career than the other services, but spreads promotions to O-10 across more years than the other services. Promotion of Marine Corps officers to O-10 occurs within a 3-year range.

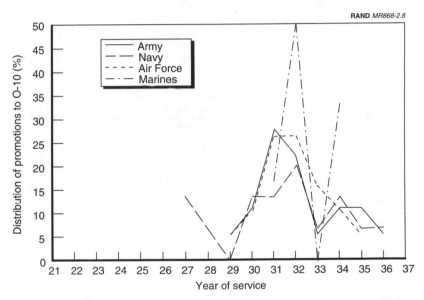

Figure 2.8—Distribution of Promotions to Grade O-10

Distribution of Promotions by Service and Year of Service

The next four figures show the pattern of promotion by years of service within a service.

In the Army, as shown in Figure 2.9, promotions to grade O-7 cluster around the 26th year of service but spread out across many years of service. Promotions to grades O-8 and O-9 peak about 2 to 3 years after that of the previous grade. Promotions to grade O-10 spread out over a 7-year period beginning with the 29th year of ser-

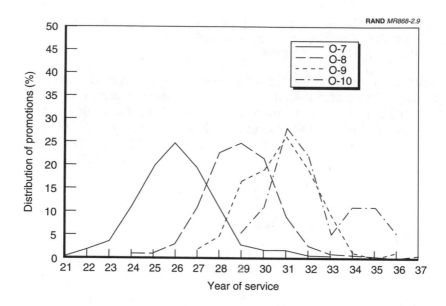

Figure 2.9—Distribution of Promotions: Army

vice. There is overlap in years of service for promotions to O-9 and O-10.

Figure 2.10 indicates that Navy promotions to all grades occur across a wide number of years of service. Years 30 and 31 see a large percentage of O-9 promotions, but these are also the peak years for O-8 promotions.[11] Also, the Navy begins to make O-10 promotions at the 27th year of service, when a significant number of promotions to lower grades are still being made. The Navy shows a pattern of simultaneous promotions (from those with similar time-in-service) being made to all grades in many years of service. As a result, the widest variation of career experience exists among Navy admirals at the various grades.

---

[11]As noted elsewhere, many Navy admirals are promoted to grade O-9 with little or no time spent at grade O-8.

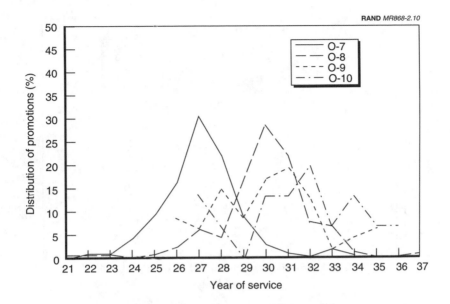

RAND *MR868-2.10*

Figure 2.10—Distribution of Promotions: Navy

In Figure 2.11, the Air Force appears to have a cyclical promotion pattern with peak activity between the four general officer grades occurring in 2- to 3-year increments.

Figure 2.12 shows that the Marine Corps also has a cyclical pattern, with the peaks occurring about 2 to 3 years apart. Moreover, the Marine Corps pattern clusters more closely around the average promotion point than do the other services.

Distribution of All Promotion Activity

These last four views portray the proportion of all promotion activity that occurs in a particular year of service for each grade and service. For these displays, the promotion activity to each grade as shown in the previous four figures is "stacked" one grade on the other to get an idea of where in a career the most promotion activity occurs. For example, as shown in Figure 2.13, the Army promotes to all four grades from those with 31 years of service. A few officers (<5 percent) with

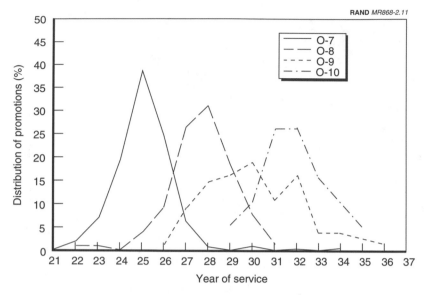

Figure 2.11—Distribution of Promotions: Air Force

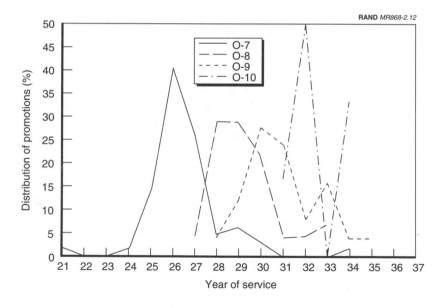

Figure 2.12—Distribution of Promotions: Marines

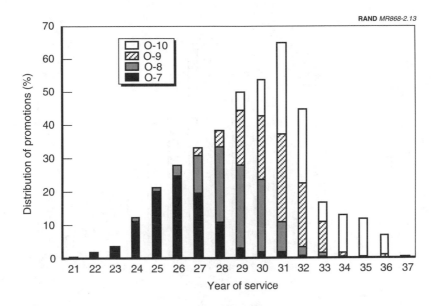

Figure 2.13—Percentage Distribution of General Officer Promotions: Army

31 years of service are promoted to O-7; about 10 percent of all O-8
promotions occur from those with 31 years of service; and about 30
percent of all promotions to both O-9 and O-10 are made from those
with 31 years of service. Most O-7 promotions occur by year 28, most
O-8 by year 31, and most O 9 and O-10 by year 34. In general, most
promotions to all grades occur between years 24 and 35

Most notable about the Navy promotion distribution, shown in Figure 2.14, is the spread of promotion activity to the four grades that
extends from year of service 27 to year of service 34. Promotion to
admiral appears to be somewhat independent of years of career experience.

Figure 2.15 indicates that the Air Force spreads the bulk of its promotion activity from the 25th to 32nd year of service, with almost all
promotions to O-7 and O-8 made before the 30th year of service. We
again observe the more cyclical pattern of Air Force promotions. The
bulk of O-7 promotions are made at years of service 25 and 26; the
bulk of O-8 promotions are made at years of service 27 and 28.

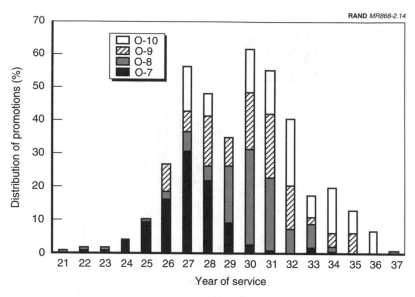

Figure 2.14—Percentage Distribution of Flag Officer Promotions: Navy

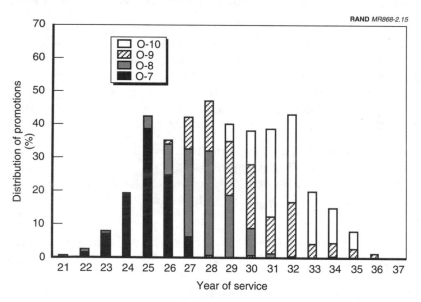

Figure 2.15—Percentage Distribution of General Officer Promotions:
Air Force

Promotions to O-9 and O-10 are spread primarily from years of service 27 through 35.

Most of the Marine Corps promotion activity, shown in Figure 2.16, takes place between the 25th and 34th year of service. Almost all promotions to O-7 are made by the 30th year of service. We observe a cyclical pattern of promotions across the four grades as years of service increase.

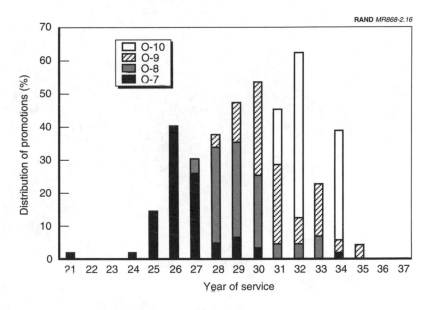

Figure 2.16—Percentage Distribution of General Officer Promotions: Marine Corps

Chapter Three

CERTAIN CONSEQUENCES OF ADDITIONAL SERVICE

The previous chapter described the quantitative information requested by Congress concerning the time-in-grade when selected for
promotion, the length of time spent on promotion lists, and the tour
lengths. This chapter takes up the questions of how the rate of
movement through positions influences effectiveness and what certain consequences may be of extending tenure.

CAREER PATHS AND MOBILITY

Organizations, both military and civilian, manage their executives
through career paths. A career path is a long-term series of related
positions that includes a clear pattern of systemic advancement.
Such careers are designed to make the large organization (in this case
the military service) effective by moving executives along these paths
to give them experiences that develop the leadership and management skills required later. Individuals have to serve in these positions long enough to acquire these skills, to test their ability to move
up, and to make the subordinate organizations effective while they
are in them. The primary emphasis in moving over these paths falls
on the number of positions that should be held, their variety
(breadth), and the length of service in each (depth). The amount of
mobility through these paths varies across time periods and organizations.[1] Some time periods and some organizations are character-

---

[1]Some of this discussion is drawn from H. Dudley Dewhirst, "Career Patterns:
Mobility, Specialization, and Related Career Issues," in Robert F. Morrison and Jerome

ized by high mobility rates.[2] Many organizations have consciously chosen to slow the rate of movement in more recent times.

Mobility in the form of job rotation is a management development tool used in most organizations, but there is little evidence about optimum mobility rates among managers. In particular, cause and effect are difficult to sort out: Does mobility enhance performance or does performance enhance mobility? A study by H. Dudley Dewhirst suggests, "It may well be that more frequent moves are appropriate for managers because managerial positions in general require less specialized knowledge than the typical science/engineering position. Optimum tenure in such positions may be more a function of the potentially dysfunctional effects of rapid mobility on the organization."[3]

There is a generalized assertion in the career literature that more time in a position improves individual and organizational performance. The theory is that when a person enters into a new position, there is a learning curve that must be followed. During this learning of the job, performance is less than when the job has been mastered. However, too much time in a job might lead to indifferent or unresponsive performance, an unwillingness to make needed organizational change, or entrenchment based on personal loyalties that might conflict with organizational priorities. A small body of empirical evidence about tenure in and through positions exists.[4] In the military, the high rate of job rotation has been attributed not only to legal constraints but also to the desire to emphasize multiple experiences and career progression, which limits the development of deep experience in major jobs. In general, senior military officers move through positions faster (see Table 2.3) than do executives in other organizations.[5]

Adams, eds., *Contemporary Career Development Issues*, Hillsdale, NJ: Lawrence Erlbaum Associates, Pub., 1991, pp. 73–107.

[2]For example, for a long time, IBM employees jokingly referred to the company acronym as standing for "I've Been Moved."

[3]Dewhirst, *loc. cit.*

[4]Dewhirst, *loc. cit.*

[5]Dewhirst suggests the optimum ranges for assignments are from about 3 years at a minimum to as long as 10 years at a maximum. Much of the empirical data cited is for engineers and scientists; there is less evidence about managers. Peter Drucker has as-

In our assessment, we show the consequences of additional allowed service on the number and variety of positions in which an officer can serve and on the length of time in such positions. In our conclusions, we evaluate the relative benefits and drawbacks of this additional service.

APPROACHES TO ADDITIONAL SERVICE

We assess the consequences of changing the current policy requiring general officers to retire upon completion of 35 years of service. We do this by adding 5 years of service in various ways and observing both systemic and career-path consequences. It is not enough simply to change the policy and allow general and flag officers to serve to 40 years of commissioned service. Our focus is not on the 40-year career. Instead, we focus on the actual amount of additional time served as a general officer and what actually happens during the added time. Note that removing the 35-year cap does not require the services to manage any differently; it simply provides an opportunity to manage routinely in ways they cannot now.[6]

For example, one way to implement the policy would be to allow all O-10s to serve routinely for 5 more years.[7] If their average years in grade were now 4.5, we would have them serve on average for 9.5 years. Another way to implement the policy would be to allocate the 5 years across all grades. For example, O-7 to O-9 would serve on average for an additional year each and O-10 would serve for 2 additional years. In this case, overall time served as a flag-rank officer

---

serted that 5 years overall is about right. One year to learn the job; 3 years to do it; and 1 year to prepare for and seek the next job. John Welch, CEO of General Electric Co., has stated that a CEO requires 15 years of tenure: 5 years to get into the swing and at least 10 more to impose a vision. This suggests CEOs need to be in place by age 50 in order to have a long run in office. (Dyan Machan, "Junior Achievement," *Forbes*, May 5, 1997, p. 44.) In a 1981 study, Veiga estimates that managers change positions every 3 and one-half years but there is considerable variation with 5 percent moving in 18 months and 5 percent moving only once in 12 years. Additionally, Fiedler (1996) advocates that the situation matters in all studies of the value of experience. In particular, Fiedler cites empirical studies that show that the value of experience depends on the stressfulness of the situation. Under stressful conditions, experience and performance are positively correlated.

[6]If there are underlying problems with assignment and promotion practices, changing the allowed tenure system would not necessarily solve them.

[7]As noted earlier, the services can seek such exceptions now and do so selectively.

would increase by the 5 years. A third way to implement the change would be to allow additional service to certain positions at certain grades but not to all. There are many other possible ways that the change could be implemented, and each would have a different effect on the breadth or depth of experience gained. We will be explicit in our assessment about how we are adding additional time because it is germane to the consequences.

In our assessment, we retain the assumption (now in law) that officers not promoted after 5 years would retire.[8] Only those with continuing prospects for advancement are allowed to continue for the additional service. In assessing career path consequences, we place emphasis upon officers who are likely to be promoted to higher general and flag officer grades. If the purpose of these additional years were to derive more service from officers who were not going to be promoted to higher grades, and if we chose not to retain the above assumption (limiting time-in-grade to 5 years), then in the most extreme case, policy and law could change to permit additional years to be served in grades O-7, O-8, O-9, and O-10. This case would assume that officers who would take advantage of the additional 5 years in any grade would most likely not be promoted to the next higher grade. If this tenure model were accompanied by assignment policies that retained these officers in assignments for longer periods of time, then this policy would increase the stability of leadership in organizations at the cost of severely constrained promotion opportunity. For the purposes of this limited study, we do not pursue this type of policy change and instead limit the years added within any of the general and flag officer grades to a sum of 5, which is most likely to have those officers who will reach the grade of O-10 reaching age 62.

------

[8]Mandatory points in law generally occur at 5 years of service in each grade. Moreover, it is common to have "gentlemen's agreements" whereby officers voluntarily retire before 5 years of service when it becomes clear that they are not competitive for further advancement. However, officers, particularly in grade O-8, who are promoted to that grade prior to the 30th year of service could continue to serve until their 35th year. In general, organizations are moving away from age- or experience-based decisions about groups of people and making decisions about individuals and their performance.

TYPES OF CONSEQUENCES

We assess the consequences of adding 5 years to general and flag officer careers from two perspectives: systemic and career path. The systemic consequences appear in the different promotion rates and time-in-grade patterns that might result from 5 years of additional actual service. The career-path consequences represent the more complex issues of how career paths—that is, number and length of assignments—might change with an additional 5 years.

Systemic Consequences

The systemic consequences can be derived from relatively simple mathematical relationships, based on proportions of officers at a particular grade and the average length of service at that grade.[9] These mathematical relationships underlie the steady-state planning models that many manpower analysts use (see Appendix C). Adding 5 years to the officer careers has different effects upon the promotion rate and the time-in-grade, depending upon how the time is applied. This analysis considers six options:

- A base case. This is the status quo and provides the basis of comparison.

- Add 5 years to the careers of O-10s. This is similar to the way the current waivers affect careers, but here the additional 5 years applies to all O-10s, rather than a selected minority.

- Apply 5 years across all the flag-rank officer grades by increasing the average time-in-grade of O-7 through O-9 by 1 year and

_____

[9]We make steady-state assessments, i.e., how the system would operate after transition has occurred. In the steady-state system, the total number (distribution) of officers at a particular grade does not change. The number of officers exiting a grade annually equals the number of officers entering the grade in that same period. Thus, promotions to O-7 equal the promotions to O-8 plus the number of O-7 officers leaving the military without being promoted. In addition, the number of officers entering (or leaving) a grade is equal to the total number of officers at that grade divided by the average time in that grade. The average time-in-grade can be calculated by dividing the total number of officers at that grade by the annual number of promotions to that grade.

O-10s by 2 years.[10] This option is consistent with giving officers deeper experience.

•   Add 5 years at the grade of O-8, which is consistent with broadening experience at that grade.

•   Add 2.5 years to O-7 and O-8, which allows them to have broader or deeper experience at these grades.

•   Add 2 years to O-7 and O-8 and 1 year to O-9.

To determine the general systemic consequences displayed, we use numbers and grade distributions that generally approximate all services. Grade distributions (e.g., 50 percent at O-7, 35 percent at O-8) are common among the services as are times-in-grade. The relative changes in promotion tempo and time-in-grade do not change with changes in the overall number of flag-rank officers in the system. That is, the results hold for the Army, Navy, Air Force, and Marines, even with different numbers of general and flag officers (Table 3.1), given the consistent proportions of general and flag officers at each grade and reasonably similar times-in-grade in the base case.

We explored the systemic consequences of variations in career tenure with six different cases. The following text describes the cases and discusses the results, which are shown in Table 3.2.

Table 3.1

Authorized Flag-Rank Positions by Grade

	Number					Percent		
	O-7	O-8	O-9	O-10	Total	O-7	O-8	O-9-10
Army	151	106	34	11	302	50	35	15
Air Force	140	98	31	10	279	50	35	15
Navy	108	76	24	8	216	50	35	15
Marine Corps	34	24	8	2	68	50	35	15

---

[10]We also explored the consequence if additional early retirement were to occur at certain grades as promotion rates decreased. For increases in the numbers of retirements of up to 25 percent, significant change in promotion rates or time-in-grade were not observed.

Base Case—Current Practice. This system has general and flag officers distributed as follows: 50 percent O-7; 35 percent O-8; and 15 percent O-9 and O-10. On average, officers serve 3.5 years in each of the grades O-7 to O-9 and 4.5 years in grade O-10. Annual promotion rates to the three highest grades, the proportion of those who enter a grade who reach the next higher grade (promotion probability), and the cumulative promotion probability to O-10 are shown in the table.

The other cases are variations of the base case. The same number and distribution of flag-rank officers are used for every case. For all cases, we lift the 35-year service limit. In the first three variations we retain the 5-years-in-grade tenure. In the fourth variation, only O-8 serve for up to 8 years in grade; in the final two cases we allow all to serve up to 6 years in grade.

Case 2—Longer O-10. This case adds 5 years to the time-in-grade for O-10s. Increasing time-in-service for O-10 has the greatest effect on annual promotions to O-10, which decrease by slightly over 50 percent. Some minor impact trickles down to O-9 and O-8 promotions. In a similar fashion, only O-10s experience significant increase in time-in-grade. Somewhat lower annual rates of promotion occur. While the same number of O-7s reach O-8, fewer who reach O-8 reach O-9 and far fewer who reach O-9 reach O-10. So for the same number of officers, O-10s serve longer and fewer officers eventually get promoted to O-10. The number and distribution of flag-rank officers remain unchanged; only the tempo of the system changes.

Case 3—Longer Service, All General and Flag Officer Grades. Case 3 adds 1 year each to grades O-7, O-8, and O-9 and 2 years to the time-in-grade as an O-10. In this case, the decrease in annual number of promotions spreads more evenly across all grades. From 20 to 29 percent fewer promotions are made to each grade, and time at each grade increases by approximately 25 percent (38 percent more for O-10). While increasing selectivity, the fewer promotions to O-7 will limit the number of officers who have the opportunity to serve as a general or flag officer.[11] Annual promotion rates decline, but over time, approximately the proportion of those who reach the next higher grade equals that in the base case. The reason for this

---

[11]As stated earlier, change in promotions from the grade of O-6 could have effects for the O-1 to O-6 officer management system.

apparent anomaly—declining rate but same proportion of promotion—is that while fewer promotions to a grade occur each year, the base for calculating the opportunity to the next grade is also smaller. Eventually, proportionally as many who reach a grade reach the next higher grade as in the base case. On average, officers have more experience when promoted and serve in grade longer. The trade-off in this case is between experience and annual promotions; promotion probability over time stays the same for reaching the three highest grades because the number entering grade O-7 is smaller.

Case 4—Longer O-8. This case adds 5 years to the time-in-grade as an O-8. Changes in promotion tempo and time-in-grade in this case are limited to grades O-7 and O-8. The O-7 effect trickles down from adding the 5 years to O-8 tenure. Higher grades are not affected. (As a general rule, changes in time-in-grade only affect grades at and below where the change is made.) The number of annual promotions to O-8 in this case is cut in half, while the length of time-in-grade more than doubles. The annual promotion rate to O-8 drops considerably, from 20 percent to 9 percent. Annual promotion rates to O-9 and O-10 do not change. (The same number of O-9s and O-10s are promoted and the base numbers of O-8 and O-9 do not change.) Over time, a little over one-third of those who make O-7 will make O-8, but almost three-quarters of those who make O-8 will get promoted to O-9. The bottleneck in promotions is to grade O-8; fewer get through it than in the base case. In this case, the overall effect is that the pool of officers at the grade of O-8 is very experienced when selected for O-9. Far fewer O-7s get promoted to O-8 each year. Those who do serve much longer at the grade of O-8.

Case 5—Longer O-7 and O-8. Case 5 adds 2.5 years each to grades O-7 and O-8. The decrease in promotion tempo and increase in time-in-grade spread more evenly between O-7 and O-8 than in case 4. Fewer annual promotions are made to O-7 and O-8 than in the base case, but the bottleneck at O-8 in the previous case disappears. Time-in-grade for O-7 and O-8 increases significantly. Promotion probability to O-8 and especially to O-9 is high compared to the base case. The overall effect is fewer promotions to O-7 and O-8, but more experienced officers in grades O-7 and O-8.

Case 6—Longer O-7, O-8, and O-9. Case 6 spreads the additional 5 years across the three lower general and flag officer grades by adding 2 years each to grades O-7 and O-8 and 1 year to grade O-9. Promotion tempo is reduced in the first three grades, while time-in-grade climbs. Over time, grade-to-grade promotion probabilities to the three highest grades increase from the base case, reflecting the smaller absolute number who get promoted from grade to grade.

The columns in Table 3.2 show the changes that occur when compared with a base case in terms of different attributes. The fundamental trade-off occurs between high promotion tempo and longer tenure in grade, which enables career-path changes. The first two columns show the percent change from the base case. Column 1 is the change in time-in-grade, and column 2 is the change in the number of promotions that occur as time-in-grade changes. The last three columns show three rates of progression. Column 3 is the promotion rate of progression and uses the number of flag-rank officers in grade as a base.[12] The denominator is constant for all cases (the number of flag-rank officers does not change in our analysis), so the rate is driven by the numerator, the number of officers promoted. Columns 4 and 5 use the number of officers promoted as a base. This denominator does change for different cases. Column 4 shows the likelihood of promotion from the previous grade, and column 5 shows the eventual likelihood of promotion from O-7.

Career-Path Consequences

The systemic consequences are average system responses to certain changes in time spent in a grade. Besides these quantitative systemic consequences, career-path consequences could also result from adding 5 years to the careers of individual flag-rank officers. Additional time spent in a grade needs to be considered in terms of

---

[12]The steady-state number of officers promoted to the next grade can be calculated by the number of officers at the next grade, divided by the length of time they spend at that grade. Thus, the promotion rate for O-7s to O-8 is the number of O-8s, divided by the average time-in-grade at O-8, divided by the total number of O-7s, in order to determine a rate. The number who retire are assumed constant. Retirement rates would probably change as promotions change, but we had no basis for predicting this change. Time-in-grade can change as promotions and retirements increase or decrease.

Table 3.2

Systemic Consequence of Changes to Length of Service in Grade

	Percent		Rates		
	% Change in Time-in-Grade	% Change Annual Promotions to Grade Shown	Annual Promotion Rate to Grade Shown (%)	Promotion Probability to Grade Shown (%)	Eventual Promotion Probability from Grade O-7 (%)
Base Case					
O-7	—	—	—	—	—
O-8	—	—	20	69	69
O-9	—	—	9	32	22
O-10	—	—	7	26	6
Case 2. Add 5 years to O-10					
O-7	0	0	—	—	—
O-8	1	−1	20	69	69
O-9	5	−5	9	31	21
O-10	99	−51	4	14	3
Case 3. Add 1,1,1,2 years to O-7 to O-10					
O-7	26	−22	—	—	—
O-8	25	−20	17	71	71
O-9	24	−21	8	32	23
O-10	38	−29	5	23	5
Case 4. Add 5 years to O-8					
O-7	13	−12	—	—	—
O-8	121	−55	9	36	36
O-9	0	0	10	71	26
O-10	0	0	7	26	7
Case 5. Add 2.5 years to O-7 and O-8					
O-7	71	−42	—	—	—
O-8	56	−36	13	77	77
O-9	0	0	10	51	39
O-10	0	0	7	26	10
Case 6. Add 2,2,1 years to O-7 to O-9					
O-7	56	−36	—	—	—
O-8	48	−32	14	74	74
O-9	21	−18	8	39	29
O-10	0	−0	7	31	9

NOTE: Promotion rates to O-7 are not shown because such rates depend also on the numbers of O-6s, which we have not estimated.

numbers and duration of assignments. Part of this analysis is based upon the premise that officers promoted to O-10 have different career paths and assignment patterns from other officers. In other words, officers who will become O-10s distinguish themselves early, fill different kinds of assignments for different periods of time, and get promoted faster than do other officers. This understanding is necessary in order to analyze how best to use an extra 5 years and to distinguish between using these additional years to get more out of the very best officers—those who become O-10s—or to change the use of general/flag officers as a set.

Trunk and Branch Model. We used an underlying conceptual flow model of general and flag careers from which to assess analytically changes in overall time allowed. This generalized career pattern, called "trunk and branch," can be distinguished from the traditional vertical pattern that characterizes the current officer management system in the grades of O-1 to O-6. In trunk and branch (best visualized by the trunk and branches of a tree), career patterns begin at the base of the trunk but have multiple opportunities for branching into different functions or specialties. A branch assignment leads to little or no opportunity for promotion. Some jobs appear to fall between trunk and branch assignments; we label these "maybe" positions.

Both individuals and organizations have choice and flexibility. As the Dewhirst study claims, "Individuals can influence their career path so as to avoid blockages and/or achieve a better match between their interests and their work. Organizations can shift their human resources more easily, and provide alternative paths for individuals."[13] However, in this model some branches do not extend very far or get clogged, and as a result, officers leave as their expectations diminish or when they reach the mandatory 5-year tenure points. On the trunk, competition for advancement continues to the highest grade, but such advancement is limited because of the high number of individuals competing for fewer positions as the organizational pyramid narrows. Immobile seniors can block upward mobility. The line of progression in positions is generally understood, and individuals calculate their likelihood of advancement and make decisions accordingly. If they calculate low probabilities, individual officers may

---

[13]Dewhirst, p. 85.

choose to leave. If not selected for advancement, officers may find statutory limits force separation. We will use this trunk and branch conceptual model because the trunk represents the path to important positions.

Besides having different kinds of assignments, officers who become O-10s move more quickly through assignments along the career path. Tables 3.3 through 3.6 show the average assignment lengths at the grades of O-7, O-8, and O-9 for all general/flag officers compared with the average assignment length for eventual O-10s.[14] The data show that O-10s generally have shorter tours. The Navy data show two entries for eventual O-10s because some serve O-8 tours and some do not.

Breadth and Depth in Career-Path Changes

Lengthening the careers of general and flag officers by 5 years could serve two possible intents concerning assignments. Officers could gain additional depth in their careers, or they could gain additional breadth. Additional depth would come from spending more time in each assignment or in particular assignments, whereas breadth would come from experiencing more assignments.

Of the cases evaluated in the discussion of systemic results, case 3— add time to each grade—is the only case that adds only depth to the

Table 3.3

Average Assignment Lengths in Months (Army)

	O-7	O-8	O-9
All officers	19.4	24.3	27.3
Eventual O-10s	19.0	20.2	20.7

---

[14]The data for eventual O-10s shown in Tables 3.3 through 3.6 are derived from the bios of officers who served as Army, Navy, and Air Force O-10s within the past 5 years, and Marine O-10s within the past 10 years. The data for all officers were provided by the services, and include all assignment changes for general and flag officers from FY 91 to FY 95, as requested by Congress.

Table 3.4

Average Assignment Lengths in Months (Air Force)

	O-7	O-8	O-9
All officers	24.4	27.1	29.5
Eventual O-10s	17.9	22.2	23.5

Table 3.5

Average Assignment Lengths in Months (Navy)

	O-7	O-8	O-9
All officers	23	25.7	26.5
Eventual O-10, No O-8 (38%)	20.8	N/A	27.7
Eventual O-10, O-8 Tour (52%)	18.9	20.3	23.2

Table 3.6

Average Assignment Lengths in Months (Marine Corps)

	O-7	O-8	O-9
All officers	20	21.8	19.6
Eventual O-10s	20.2	22.7	18.8

NOTE: The Marine Corps data are skewed by the small sample size of eventual O-10s. There are several eventual O-10s who spent considerable time as O-7s or O-8s, but the premise of shorter tours for this population, on average, otherwise holds true.

Table 3.7

Average Number of Assignments in Grade, Eventual O-10s

	O-7	O-8	O-9	O-10	Total
Army	2	1.3	1.3	1.4	6
Air Force	2	1.7	2	1.4	7.1
Navy	1.9	.8	1.4	1.4	5.5
Marine Corps	1.7	1.8	1.1	1.1	5.7

career path.[15] This depth, however, would affect all flag officers at all grades. This case adds 1 year to the time in grade of O-7s, O-8s, and O-9s, and 2 years to the grade of O-10. Increasing the depth of experience of officers reduces the number of reassignment moves they undergo and increases the stability within individual organizations, because the general officers would stay with an organization longer. Table 3.7 shows the average number of assignments at each grade for eventual O-10s of all the services. Dividing the number of assignments at each level into the additional 5 years spread across all the assignments these officers complete as general and flag officers, each assignment would increase by approximately 10 months for the Army, 8 months for the Air Force, 11 months for the Navy, and 10.5 months for the Marine Corps.

While this additional time in these assignments increases the stability of organizations, it decreases the number of general and flag officers who have that valuable experience. Thus, because this extra time in assignments results from extra time-in-grade, fewer promotions to that grade occur.

Case 4, which adds 5 years to the time-in-grade at the grade of O-8, is designed to add breadth to the general and flag officer career path. Each officer would have more assignments at that grade from which to gain experience important to the professional demands at O-9 and O-10. The value of this experience would depend upon the type of assignments that were added to the individual's career path. If an eventual O-10 were exposed to an increased number of trunk positions, this situation might provide valuable experience to a small number of quality officers.   However, if eventual O-10s are instead exposed to an increased number of maybe positions, then there might not be value in this policy from the individual perspective. On the other hand, there might be some value from a service perspective of increasing the number of individuals who have gained additional experience of a type they do not now receive. This extra time spent within a grade would decrease the number of promotions to that grade. The extra time spent at O-8 would not necessarily have implications from the perspective of organizational stability because offi-

---

[15]Assuming that the services do not use the extra time within each of the grades to add another assignment.

cers could remain in their assignments for as long (or as short) as they do currently.

The remaining cases could add either breadth or depth to the career paths. Cases 5 and 6 both distribute the additional 5 years across multiple grades. The number of years added at any grade is sufficient to either spend more time in the current number of assignments, and thus add depth, or gain additional assignments, and thus add breadth, to the career path.

Case 2, which adds 5 years to O-10s, could add either breadth or depth. However, it differs from the other cases in that the population to which it is applied could vary. Given that O-10s distinguish themselves early and are assigned to trunk positions, different strategies for applying these 5 years to the career path are possible. First, the additional 5 years could be applied to all officers who reach O-10. This is similar to the current waiver system, except that all O-10s would lengthen their careers, rather than just those selected by the services.[16] This is the most simple implementation of this case, and this is the variation used to calculate the systemic numbers in the preceding analysis.

For a second approach, the services could select individual officers to remain in the service for up to 5 years beyond the current 35 years. This approach would produce a system much like the current one, but one in which the services do not need to request waivers to extend the careers of specific officers. The Army currently uses waivers only to provide the occasional O-10 with time to finish a current assignment, and the Navy has stated an intent not to request more than three waivers annually. All of the services stated that they have had no problems with the current waiver policy.

Another way to apply these additional 5 years for O-10s is based on the trunk and branch model. If the intent is to improve either the breadth or depth of the very best officers, those who reach O-10, the

---

[16]The services expressed concern that selecting assignments for O-10s who had already filled prominent assignments, such as Chief of Staff or commander in chief (CINC), would be difficult. However, this latter issue would be problematic only during the transition period. New O-10s would probably not receive those assignments, but would probably fill them only as their final career assignment, thus alleviating this concern.

assignments and experiences perceived to be the most valuable to these officers for development are those at more junior general and flag ranks. These best officers could increase their time at lower grades. If the best general officers distinguish themselves early and thus are filling trunk positions, then the additional years could be applied to the select group of officers in some identified billets. This group would likely include more than just the eventual O-10s, because the trunk assignments at O-7 include more officers than eventual O-8s in trunk assignment and many more than eventual O-10s. Applying these additional career years to the trunk positions would mean that the length of these assignments would increase, so that officers destined for almost certain promotion would gain more depth of experience in their career path.

This approach would require acceptance by the services, even though it may only make explicit what is implicitly known: Certain assignments lead to the top positions. Also, given the current emphasis on "fast-tracking" those with the greatest potential, this application would appear to slow the careers of those same officers. However, because of the additional time-in-grade, all promotion patterns would change and fast-tracking could still occur relative to the overall cohort of general and flag officers. Lastly, if officers spend more time in those trunk assignments, fewer would gain the experience of that valuable assignment. Keeping officers in important positions longer means that fewer have access to them. The size of the pool from which to choose would go down. Careful early selection would be required.

A relative effect upon the services needs to be considered with this implementation. The Navy reportedly has experienced the most problems developing flag officers with adequate experience to compete with officers from other services for important joint assignments. This problem has been attributed to the limited amount of time that Navy admirals have as flag officers before reaching 35 years of service and thus the relative weakness of their resumes compared to those from other services. However, even if an additional 5 years were applied to all officers, this measure would be unlikely to resolve the Navy's problem. Unless the Navy changes its career paths prior to promotion to flag officer, the additional 5 years may not resolve its quandary. By lengthening the careers of all officers, those from other services would still have relatively more experience when they were considered for four-star assignments. Instead of leveling the playing field, this application of additional years would simply lengthen it for all, including the Navy.[17]

---

[17]However, if the issue is having sufficient experience to be competitive rather than being comparable in experience, then adding 5 years would allow for more experience compared with now. Moreover, the Navy would not be up against the 35-year limit and would not have to speed their officers through the O-7 and O-8 grades.

Chapter Four

CONCLUSIONS

The objective of the 1980 DOPMA legislation with respect to general and flag officer management was to increase the time they served. DOPMA also strove to integrate field-grade careers with flag-rank careers. Since DOPMA was implemented, the environment has changed significantly to include requirements for additional assignments (e.g., for service with the reserve components or for joint tours), which are putting pressure on the lengths of all officer careers in the military.

Requiring general or flag officers to retire at 35 years of service has two types of consequences: systemic and career path. The systemic consequences of allowing longer service in one or several grades mean that fewer of those in lower grades will be promoted in any given year and fewer will rise to the highest two grades. However, this longer service increases time-in-grade between promotions, which could increase stability in assignments and the experience of those who eventually do get promoted. The number of general and flag officers in the service does not change. The consequences are that given a fixed number of officers, fewer are promoted and those who are promoted serve longer.

Career-path consequences are less predictable and depend on how a service chooses to assign flag-rank officers to use the available time. Potentially, a service could choose among extremes of continuing O-10s for much longer service and additional assignments, or continuing all general and flag officers for somewhat longer service and somewhat longer time in each assignment. This analysis placed its emphasis on those officers who would be promoted to the next higher grade, and thus it limited the total of additional years added to any grade to 5 years. Given this constraint, many other options between these explored cases still exist, including allowing only officers who are most likely to reach the grade of O-10 to serve longer in assignments.

Under the assumption that the current number and variety of assignments for officers would continue without change because that is the least radical change in career paths, officers on these career paths would serve in assignments for about 25 percent longer than they do now. More depth of experience would be the result. Alternatively, additional assignments (more breadth) could be added to the career path with assignment length continuing as is or reducing slightly.

Congress has asked whether it is appropriate to require flag-rank officers to retire after 35 years of commissioned service. Provisions already exist to continue individual general and flag officers beyond 35 years of service, and the military departments routinely but sparingly exercise these exceptions. The fact that they exist and are used answers the narrow question. Officers can and do serve beyond 35 years. The larger question is whether making this the rule rather than the exception is the better course of action. Removing the limit would not necessarily lengthen time between promotions or assignments. The services could use the same career patterns that they do now.

We believe the answer depends on three perspectives: that of the individual, that of the organizations in which general and flag officers serve, and that of the military service whose broad interests the general and flag officers serve over time. We assess those perspectives given a likely implementation of additional time—greater length in existing assignments (depth) rather than the introduction of more assignments (breadth) in the career path.

For the first perspective, we have no evidence of how individual general and flag officers would behave if allowed to serve longer overall and in each assignment. Officers may continue to behave as they do now. They would seek advancement to positions of responsibility, would serve as long as they were contributing, and would retire when not competitive or after 5 years of service in grade as they do now.

From their perspective, they would serve in the same positions in which they do now but for somewhat longer periods. Fewer officers on average would be promoted to higher grades, and there would be greater time periods between promotions. Certain officers would be assigned to positions with greater likelihood of continued advancement, as they are now, and these officers would advance relatively more quickly than the service average.

In terms of the second perspective, the organizations (i.e., specific commands) in which general and flag officers serve would probably benefit because their leaders would serve for somewhat longer periods. Again, the same officers as now would be assigned to the same organizational positions as now, but there would be less turnover within the organization. The organizations would not be aware that promotions had slowed; they would be aware that lengths of service had increased for those general and flag officers assigned to them. Organizations would be better off to the extent that less movement than now would probably improve organizational performance. Greater length in assignments, up to a point, is generally accepted as preferable for individual and organizational effectiveness.

Third, from the perspective of the military service, the pool of officers competing for the positions of highest responsibility (moving from grade to grade) would be smaller but more experienced. It is not clear whether a service ultimately prizes depth or breadth of experience. Under our implementation assumption, the same breadth of experience would occur but with deeper experience in each assignment, which is a benefit. Overall, fewer officers would have had the opportunity to gain these experiences, which is a disadvantage. The trade-off for the service would be a smaller but more experienced pool of competitors for advancement.

Ultimately then, the answer to the question posed about the appropriateness of mandatory retirement of certain officers after 35 years of commissioned service rests in objectives. For example, if the desired outcome is greater stability overall and in particular organizations, then lifting the 35-year limit and allowing officers to serve longer in all assignments would accomplish that. If the objective is rapid movement along a career path to more important positions, then the current system accomplishes that. If the objective is to reap the benefit from having developed officers by allowing them to serve longer, then removing the 35-year limit seems best. These objectives, and others that might be put forward, sometimes conflict with each other, and decisionmakers need to decide which are the most important.

LEGISLATION PERTAINING TO GENERAL OR FLAG OFFICER TENURE

The legislation pertinent to tenure for general or flag officers appears in Title 10 U.S. Code, Sections 635, 636 and 637. Relevant portions are quoted below.

10 USC Sec. 635

Except as provided under section 637(b) of this title, each officer of the Regular Army, Regular Air Force, or Regular Marine Corps who holds the regular grade of brigadier general, and each officer of the Regular Navy who holds the regular grade of rear admiral (lower half), who is not on a list of officers recommended for promotion to the regular grade of major general or rear admiral, respectively, shall, if not earlier retired, be retired on the first day of the first month beginning after the date of the fifth anniversary of his appointment to that grade or on the first day of the month after the month in which he completes 30 years of active commissioned service, whichever is later.

10 USC Sec. 636

Except as provided under section 637(b) of this title, each officer of the Regular Army, Regular Air Force, or Regular Marine Corps who holds the regular grade of major general, and each officer of the Regular Navy who holds the regular grade of rear admiral, shall, if not earlier retired, be retired on the first day of the first month beginning after the date of the fifth anniversary of his appointment to that grade or on the first day of the month after the month in which he completes 35 years of active commissioned service, whichever is later.

10 USC Sec. 637

An officer subject to retirement under section 635 or 636 of this title who is serving in the grade of brigadier general, rear admiral (lower half), major general, or rear admiral may, subject to the needs of the service, have his retirement deferred and be continued on active duty by the Secretary concerned. An officer subject to retirement under section 635 or 636 of this title who is serving in a grade above major general or rear admiral may have his retirement deferred and be continued on active duty by the President.

Any deferral of retirement and continuation on active duty under this subsection shall be for a period not to exceed five years, but such period may not (except as provided under section 1251(b) of this title) extend beyond the date of the officer's sixty-second birthday.

10 USC Sec. 1251

(a) Unless retired or separated earlier, each regular commissioned officer of the Army, Navy, Air Force, or Marine Corps (other than an officer who is a permanent professor, director of admissions, or registrar of the United States Military Academy or United States Air Force Academy or a commissioned warrant officer) shall be retired on the first day of the month following the month in which he becomes 62 years of age. An officer who is a permanent professor at the United States Military Academy or United States Air Force Academy, the director of admissions at the United States Military Academy, or the registrar of the United States Air Force Academy shall be retired on the first day of the month following the month in which he becomes 64 years of age.

(b) Notwithstanding subsection (a), the President may defer the retirement of an officer serving in a position that carries a grade above major general or rear admiral, but such a deferment may not extend beyond the first day of the month following the month in which the officer becomes 64 years of age. Not more than ten deferments of retirement under this subsection may be in effect at any one time.

SERVICE DATA

This appendix provides the specific data requested by Congress. This data was provided by each of the military services.

Table B.1

Average Time-in-Grade at the Time of Selection (Years), Army

Competitive Category and Grade	FY91	FY92	FY93	FY94	FY95
Army Competitive Category (ACC)					
O-7	3.2	2.9	3.3	3.2	3.4
O-8	1.7	1.6	1.8	1.8	1.7
Judge Advocate General's Corps (JA)					
O-7		2.3		3.6	
Chaplain Corps (CH)					
O-7	7.1			7.3	
Medical Corps (MC)					
O-7	9.5	9.1	8.1	9.5	9.5
O-8	1.7		3.2		2.6
Dental Corps (DC)					
O-7				5.8	
Medical Service Corps (MS)					
O-7		3.1			
Army Nurse (AN)					
O-7	2.8				2.6

Table B.2

Average Time-in-Grade at the Time of Selection (Years), Air Force

Competitive Category and Grade	FY91	FY92	FY93	FY94	FY95
Line					
O-7	6.1	4.5	5.1	4.7	4.7
O-8	2.4	1.4	2.1	2.0	2.0
Judge Advocate General's Corps (JAG)					
O-7		6.7	8.8	9.2	7.2
O-8					1.5
Chaplain Corps (CHAP)					
O-7		6.0			5.9
O-8	2.9			1.3	
Senior Health Care Executive (HP)					
O-7		8.3	6.0	9.6	9.9
O-8		3.1	3.3	2.9	

Table B.3

Average Time-in-Grade at the Time of Selection (Years), Navy

Competitive Category and Grade	FY91	FY92	FY93	FY94	FY95
Unrestricted Line (URL)					
O-7	5.0	5.0	5.0	5.3	5.0
O-8	1.7	1.8	2.1	1.4	1.6
Staff Corps Judge Advocate General's Corps (JAG)					
O-7	3.6				4.7
O-8				2.5	
Chaplain Corps (CHC)					
O-7	8.9				7.4
O-8	3.2				3.1
Medical Corps (MC)					
O-7	9.1	10.1	9.1	10.5	8.3
O-8	1.1	3.2	1.6	1.9	1.4
Dental Corps (DC)					
O-7		10.4			8.5
O-8					1.4
Medical Service Corps (MSC)					
O-7			6.8		
Nurse Corps (NC)					
O-7		3.7			7.1
Civil Engineer Corps (CEC)					
O-7	5.5	5.5	5.8	5.8	6.1
O-8		1.0	1.8	1.3	1.0
Supply Corps (SC)					
O-7	6.0	8.3	5.2	5.5	4.7
O-8	1.3	1.9	1.8	1.2	1.8
Restricted Line Engineering Duty (ED)					
O-7	5.4	5.3	5.9	5.6	6.3
O-8	1.4	2.1	1.9	1.5	1.9
Aerospace Engineering (AED)					
O-7	5.3	6.6	5.3	3.3	5.9
O-8	0.8		1.3	0.0	0.0
Cryptology (CRYPTO)					
O-7		5.2			5.1
O-8		1.2			
Intelligence (INTEL)					
O-7	3.2	3.8		2.7	4.1
O-8	1.3		1.0	1.0	
Public Affairs (PAO)					
O-7			2.4		
O-8					1.4
Oceanography					
O-7		5.4			6.1

Table B.4

Average Time-in-Grade at the Time of Selection (Years), Marine Corps

Competitive Category and Grade	FY91	FY92	FY93	FY94	FY95
Line					
O-7	3.5	3.5	2.9	3.3	3.4
O-8	1.4	1.8	1.4	1.8	1.8

Table B.5

Average Time-in-Grade at the Time of Promotion (Years), Army

Competitive Category and Grade	FY91	FY92	FY93	FY94	FY95
Army Competitive Category (ACC)					
O-7	5.7	4.3	3.6	4.6	4.5
O-8	3.4	3.0	3.2	3.0	3.3
O-9	2.2	2.3	2.1	2.6	2.3
O-10	1.4	3.0	2.7	2.4	2.6
Judge Advocate General's Corps (JA)					
O-7	7.7	2.5		3.9	
O-8		0.7		2.2	
Chaplain Corps (CH)					
O-7	7.3				7.6
O-8				3.8	
Medical Corps (MC)					
O-7	13.1	9.5		11.4	10.0
O-8	2.4			5.1	2.9
O-9		4.2			
Dental Corps (DC)					
O-7	7.6				7.9
O-8	4.0				3.5
Medical Service Corps (MS)					
O-7			3.4		
Army Nurse (AN)					
O-7		3.5			

Table B.6

**Average Time-in-Grade at the Time of Promotion (Years),
Air Force**

Competitive Category and Grade	FY91	FY92	FY93	FY94	FY95
Line					
O-7	6.9	5.2	5.9	5.6	6.0
O-8	3.4	2.4	3.1	3.0	3.0
O-9	4.0	2.1	2.6	3.0	2.4
O-10	2.6	3.7	3.3	3.7	3.0
Judge Advocate General's Corps (JAG)					
O-7		7.4	9.7	9.7	7.7
O-8			5.0		2.1
Chaplain Corps (CHAP)					
O-7		6.5			6.4
O-8	3.6			2.2	
Senior Health Care Executive (HP)					
O-7		9.0	7.0	10.2	10.9
O-8		3.8	4.2	3.6	
O-9				4.3	

Table B.7

Average Time-in-Grade at the Time of Promotion (Years), Navy

Competitive Category and Grade	FY91	FY92	FY93	FY94	FY95
Unrestricted Line (URL)					
O-7	6.4	6.5	6.3	6.8	6.4
O-8	3.1	2.8	2.6	2.6	3.0
O-9[a]	2.0	0.7	0.9	0.9	1.3
O-10	2.8	3.9		3.0	2.5
Staff Corps Judge Advocate General's Corps (JAG)					
O-7	3.6				4.7
O-8				2.5	
Chaplain Corps (CHC)					
O-7	8.9				8.3
O-8	3.2				3.1
Medical Corps (MC)					
O-7	10.2	11.3	9.0	12.2	11.2
O-8	1.7	3.9	2.9	3.7	3.3
O-9	1.7				2.9
Dental Corps (DC)					
O-7		12.1			10.2
O-8					3.0
Medical Service Corps (MSC) O-7			8.5		
Nurse Corps (NC)					
O-7		4.6			8.1
Civil Engineer Corps (CEC)					
O-7	6.9	6.1	6.8	7.3	7.1
O-8		1.8	2.3	3.0	2.5
Supply Corps (SC)					
O-7	7.9	9.8	6.7	7.1	6.7
O-8	2.3	3.1	3.0	2.1	3.6
O-9		0.0[b]			
Restricted Line Engineering Duty (ED)					
O-7	7.1	6.7	7.7	7.2	7.2
O-8	3.0	3.1	3.0	2.8	3.2
O-9	3.7				

Table B.7—continued

Competitive Category and Grade	FY91	FY92	FY93	FY94	FY95
Aerospace Engineering (AED)					
O-7		7.5	6.5	5.2	7.6
O-8	2.1		2.0		
O-9	0.6				
Cryptology (CRYPTO)					
O-7		7.1			7.1
O-8		2.7			
Intelligence (INTEL)					
O-7	5.0	5.2		4.8	6.4
O-8	3.1		2.0	2.6	
O-9		0.0^b			
O-10		3.3			
Public Affairs (PAO)					
O-7			3.2		
O-8					2.4
Oceanography					
O-7		6.2			7.0

[a]When the date of rank for promotion to O-8 occurred after the date of rank for O-9, zero time was credited for time-in-grade.

[b]Date of rank to O-8 was subsequent to date of rank to O-9.

Table B.8

Average Time-in-Grade at the Time of Promotion (Years), Marine Corps

Competitive Category and Grade	FY91	FY92	FY93	FY94	FY95
Line					
O-7	4.6	4.4	3.7	4.3	4.5
O-8	2.6	2.8	1.9	2.8	2.8
O-9	2.0	0.8	2.2	2.4	1.6
O-10	1.8	2.1		1.0	2.3

Table B.9

Average Tour Lengths for General or Flag Officers Who Changed Positions or Assignments (Years), Army

Grade	FY91	FY92	FY93	FY94	FY95
O-7					
Joint	1.6	1.3	1.7	1.5	2.0
Nonjoint	1.6	1.6	1.6	1.6	1.6
O-8					
Joint	1.8	1.9	2.1	2.0	2.2
Nonjoint	1.7	2.0	2.2	2.1	2.3
O-9					
Joint	2.4	2.2	2.1	1.9	1.7
Nonjoint	2.3	2.3	2.2	2.1	2.9
O-10					
Joint	1.0	5.0	4.0	2.1	0.0
Nonjoint	1.4	3.2	0.0	1.7	2.5

Table B.10

Average Tour Lengths for General or Flag Officers Who Changed Positions or Assignments (Years), Air Force

Grade	FY91	FY92	FY93	FY94	FY95
O-7					
Joint	1.9	2.1	1.6	3.0	2.3
Nonjoint	2.2	2.2	1.9	1.7	1.9
O-8					
Joint	3.3	2.2	2.3	2.5	2.8
Nonjoint	3.0	1.8	2.1	2.4	1.7
O-9					
Joint	1.9	4.2	3.3	2.5	2.9
Nonjoint	2.8	2.1	1.8	2.8	2.4
O-10					
Joint	4.5	0.0	0.0	1.8	1.0
Nonjoint	1.7	2.2	0.0	2.7	1.9

Table B.11

Average Tour Lengths for General or Flag Officers Who Changed Positions or Assignments (Years), Navy

Grade	FY91	FY92	FY93	FY94	FY95
O-7					
Joint	1.9	2.1	1.6	1.7	1.9
Nonjoint	2.2	2.0	1.9	1.9	1.9
O-8					
Joint	1.3	2.0	2.2	2.5	2.0
Nonjoint	2.0	2.2	2.0	2.0	2.6
O-9					
Joint	2.4	1.8	2.0	2.0	
Nonjoint	2.3	2.8	2.2	2.1	2.3
O-10					
Joint	2.3			2.6	2.3
Nonjoint	1.1	1.4		2.7	1.9

Table B.12

Average Tour Lengths for General or Flag Officers Who Changed Positions or Assignments (Years), Marine Corps

Grade	FY91	FY92	FY93	FY94	FY95
O-7					
Joint	2.0	2.0	1.3		1.2
Nonjoint	1.6	1.4	1.6	1.8	1.9
O-8					
Joint	2.0	2.1	1.9	2.1	1.7
Nonjoint	1.3	1.9	1.3	1.6	2.4
O-9					
Joint	1.0				1.4
Nonjoint	1.5	1.0	2.3	1.8	2.2
O-10					
Joint					
Nonjoint	4.0	2.1		2.4	4.0

DISCUSSION OF MANPOWER MODELS[1]

There are three types of personnel models that can be used each with its own concept and individual uses:

1. **Steady-state** (or static). Steady-state personnel planning models are used to study long-range personnel objectives as well as to examine the effects of changes in various personnel policy parameters. These models assume that, for long-term planning purposes, ideal and steady-state conditions will apply. Steady-state conditions are hypothetical and imply that loss rates and other planning factors do not change from year to year. The resulting force structure is in equilibrium, implying that the size and shape of the force structure within such models is not dependent on time.

2. **Dynamic.** Dynamic models are used to study the short-term effects of a given personnel policy. These models apply a given policy to today's force to show the planner the direction in which such a policy would take the force were it applied right away. Actually, the policy is applied more than once, to each successive structure, so that the planner can see where it would take the force were it adopted now and used for a given number of years.

3. **Transition.** Transition models aid the planner in moving today's force toward a specified objective over a given number of years.

---

[1]This passage is excerpted from Laura Sammis, Sidney Miller, and Herbert Shukiar, *The Officer Grade Limitations Model: A Steady-State Mathematical Model of the U.S. Air Force Officer Structure,* Santa Monica, CA: RAND, R-1632-PR, July 1975, pp. 2–3.

Whereas dynamic models successively apply a given policy to today's force to see where that policy leads (it may not lead to a desirable force structure in an acceptable span of time), transition models take today's force, a long-term objective, and a target year; the model then determines what policies should be adopted each year to reach the objective by the target year. While a steady-state model will identify the policy that will maintain a desirable force structure once it has been reached, a transition model allows the planner to investigate alternative ways of moving toward that force objective, beginning with today's officer inventory and policies.

Cymrot, Donald J., Carol S. Moore, John T. Ostlund, *The Length of Flag Careers*, Alexandria, VA: Center for Naval Analyses, CAB 95–67, September 1995.

Dewhirst, H. Dudley, "Career Patterns: Mobility, Specialization, and Related Career Issues," in Robert F. Morrison and Jerome Adams, eds., *Contemporary Career Development Issues*, Hillsdale, NJ: Lawrence Erlbaum Associates, Pub., 1991, pp. 73–107.

Fiedler, Fred E., "Research on Leadership Selection and Training: One View of the Future," *Administrative Science Quarterly*, 41, 1996, pp. 241–250.

Philpott, Tom, "The Navy's Pressure Cooker," *U.S. Naval Institute Proceedings*, May 1996, p. 50.

Rostker, Bernard, Harry J. Thie, James Lacy, Jennifer Kawata, Susanna Purnell, *The Defense Officer Personnel Management Act of 1980: A Retrospective Assessment*, Santa Monica, CA: RAND, R-4246-FMP, 1993.

Thie, Harry J., Roger A. Brown, et al., *Future Career Management Systems for U.S. Military Officers*, Santa Monica, CA: RAND, MR-470-OSD, 1994.

Thie, Harry J., Margaret C. Harrell, Roger A. Brown, Clifford M. Graf II, Mark Berends, Claire M. Levy, Jerry M. Sollinger, *A Future Officer Career Management System: An Objectives-based Design*, Santa Monica, CA: RAND, MR-788-OSD, 1997.